NIGHTHAWKS

Katherine Hastings

For Nathaniel
Looking forward to
reading your work.
Katherine
7/21/14
Napa

SPUYTEN DUYVIL
New York City

ACKNOWLEDGEMENTS

Some of the poems in this collection have been published by the
following journals and anthologies. Many thanks to the editors
of Taos Journal of Poetry and Art; Words Pictures Ideas; Ambush
Review; Argotist Review; Ahadada; New Way Media; Stanislaus
Review; Hill Tromper

Library of Congress Cataloging-in-Publication Data

Hastings, Katherine.
  [Poems. Selections]
  Nighthawks / Katherine Hastings.
     pages cm
  Includes bibliographical references.
  Poems.
  ISBN 978-0-923389-11-6
  I. Title.
  PS3608.A86145A6 2014
  811'.6--dc23
                           2013021414

for Cathy, always

CONTENTS

IV

Nighthawks

I

Central Park Zoo

Dear García Lorca,

It is worse now than when you were here.

Today I saw a llama, small and dark, alone
in its tiny pen, its barn where it is locked
up at night even smaller. Children
laughed and reached out their chubby arms
to pet it. No one could catch its pacing.
It had no one to speak llama to. Poor llama.

Down the avenue in front of a bank
I saw a woman caged in suffering. She, too,
was small and dark. She was wrapped tightly
in a gray sheet that once was white, tightly
as a straight jacket, as if it would stop
her shaking. Only her tiny claw
with its sleeping cup of coins showed.
She was on the bottom step of a bank
Her head drooped forward. That woman's body
shook and shook and shook and we all
walked past. García Lorca forgive me —
I hope she is dead.

A Holy Day in New York City

There is no sun. There is no sky.
There are no stars opening
like crystal flowers. The winter streets
are narrow alleys, sit in brick piles
stacked up, up, to wall-lock the world.
Before us, in the forever dark, each
hour has had the light erased, except
for the light clung in our fists, kept
hot in our pockets, brought yesterday
from billions of light years away.
One wonders here how many know
their names. The Lion, the Virgin, the Bear.
There, out the window, the streets — stories
and more stories below — are wet
but there is no way to know if the wind blows.
The steady voice of traffic is my ocean,
accompanies me down the mountain,
over the divide to the pacific shore.
Dogs run free there. I walk. At 92nd Street
and 3rd Avenue, the wind folds umbrellas,
breaks their spines. Take-out is held
tightly in plastic bags. A little girl in
hot pink boots searches for small lakes.
The black dog in his flouncy yellow
slicker prances down the street looking
like a sunflower. Not even tourists
mind this rain. It is nature. It is real.
They tilt their heads and open their mouths
wide, as though their lives depend on it.

Catskills

The holiness of the real
Is always there...
        —Kenneth Rexroth,
            "Time is the Mercy of Eternity"

Mid-March we hiked the road
of bear crossings and silence
up to the end where the black
rocks lay layered and capped

with snow, and under that snow
a brook poured her music. This was
the only sound. Not a bird, nothing
but cold water snaking between rocks,

rivulets spilling the long-awaited song:
Spring. Now the days grow longer,
the breeze will play over the blooming fields,
black ducks pairing in the sky. Soon

I'll home to the far sea, the long golden grass
stretching over the hills, black-spotted
dairy cows sagging their loads under oaks,
under dusk, under the plume of Milky Way,

stars flashing crystal, flashing a question:
Who will climb the Catskills, look straight up
through waves of amazement to the full
configuration, life and death indiscernible.

A Walk in the Park

All day the yellow sun falls on the hills.
Bunchgrass and blackberries pour down the slope.
Last night coyotes trotted past scattered oaks
climbing to sky, sang of the catch. *Rabbit,*

rabbit, possum, fawn. The world smells
of new blood born and spilled. Frogs pronounce
from the pond, each day fainter. Wind poppies
bend softly on the plain of mouths — spiders, bats,

rough skinned newts. A boy made in the image of
Lorca reclines beneath a laurel; turkey vultures
wheel over with wings of shredded violins.
The eyes of the world are always hungry, sponges

of fruit and fascia. Down the path through white
bones of backwoods, past Skullcap and Solomon's
Seal, I look behind, sense the half-lidded stare
of a mountain lion drowsing in dust.

Beside her, a woman sunbathes on a rug,
writes of uncomplicated peace. I heed
wildcat advice, spread my arms wide, an
expanding constellation in this small

heaven of shrinking earth, a postage stamp
of impermanent creation in a world
doomed to ruin. Last night a poet read
of mountaintop removal in West Virginia,

how his family's graveyard can be seen
legally now only from a plane, how
the coal company murdered his dog.
Are we all the same species? Here a man

plants a banyan for life, a rose for love.
There a man plans to murder you in your sleep.
I walk until the lopsided moon begins her weaving
over and under, under and over,

interlacing her lightfall of peace.
I walk until the nighthawks cry.

In a Room Over New York City

There is a tapping on the window
where a leaf should be. A rain dance
on glass. Each drop stays in place,
paralyzed by soot. Across the alley
chairs are stacked on a rooftop garden
swept of dirt. The only trees in sight
are imprisoned in pots. Stunted and lonely
their roots wind around themselves.
A broken wall lies serenely on
a buried branch. Through the window
everything is gray-mottled. Tomorrow
the sun will come. What will change?

Transients

There's some wrong, that can't be salved,
something irreversible besides aging
                    —William Matthews, *"Wrong"*

Small light bodies, the stars.
Beneath them, flashing highway signs.
Eighteen-wheelers, eighty-eyed,
plow through a thousand miles of wings,

their juices dry as brick dust in a blink.
A harsh wind, a rough assault of air,
frays the flight of night birds, burns our lips.
Down the sea cliff the long skirt of earth

vanishes in watery carving, not so slow
as before the world was warmed.
The speed of earth's decay unhinges us, we say,
stepping on the gas to get home,

wade safely into the swells of dream-illusion,
our only struggle the share of whispering sheets.
Red handed and road weary we drift off
like ice floes on the ever hungry sea.

In the background enormous rhythmic voices
break on the beach. The alarm is set and ticking.

Untitled Spring Song

Again the forms of Pythagoras
Sought the organic relations
Of stone and cloud and flower..."
        "A Living Pearl" — Kenneth Rexroth

In the sun-dried meadow pocked with oaks
nameless birds sing of renewal. Warm air
moves silently into the buds, into the skin,
into a blue-black butterfly winging past
like a wild horse. It is the light of the
largest star that calls to the multitudes
of oneness. Eagles hunt the hawks,
hawks hunt the crows, crows tug up
from the road wafers of carrion.

I sit in the gathering heat come like breath,
come like an old love. It's the first day
of spring and the clouds have freed themselves
from all the branches, from every low blade
and flown off to the land of waiting.
In new warmth we drop our clothes,
lay with the flesh of earth. Nearby
black-tailed deer chew diminishing shade.
Everything reflects the flood of light, cries
We are you, you are we, our eyes,
like stars, are mirrors.

Spring, and the wind has dropped her sabers,
has settled softly on unruly soil, on breasts of
young girls abandoning unicorns for ball-capped boys.
They gather in the whirlwind of phones and texting fingers.
Overhead, a lone woodpecker in a gnarled tree:
tap, tap, tap.

II

Fallen Leaves

after Sandy Hook

Red leaves are mounded in the cold.
Crushed by the stilled flight of them
we leave our bodies for the night sky.

Inside our chests hobby horses rock,
tiny pianos play brief, familiar tunes.
In hand-knit wools, we sit beneath

one star, then another, another ... and on.
We wait for the sun. Will it come through
our heavy sighs? Will we be cured of

this expanse — an angel apiece
burning so far out of reach?

The blossoms have opened
I close my eyes against them
so bright with color
I use my hands to burrow earth,
build dirt lilies, hailstones.

Last night I saw your body
It was dry and husk-wrapped on my lap
I saw your foot
I saw your hair brushed by evening dew
into dark streams beneath a weeping moon
Birds sang for your beauty
Your full aura remained gem-like
Sparkled your edges
like some deep-sea creature
moving through the dark

Small Angels in the Mirror

After Sandy Hook

When at a loss for an ending,
have some brown hens standing in the rain.
— Billy Collins, "The Student"

1.

Trains tilted off wooden rails sit dumbly.
Paper planes sink and sink,
never find ground

Outside the breast closed tightly,
salted streams dampen every desert grain

Small doors darken all the skies
Shut-off spaces
with solid chalked walls — far, far

Darkness dries its hands
on the emptied shore
Blowing slower, ever slower, the breeze

The earth, being the earth,
can hold no one —
neither this child
nor that
Not even a hand

Silence!
An angel carries her message to heaven

2.

And the desert came and took his name
and the stillness took his father's name
and the clear sky, a soul,
and the sea, a body

The moon, everything

3.

Once there was darkness
that had for skin
sweet butter creamed with sugar

Now it is just
darkness.
The candle
just wax.

4.

The mother says

I am never aware of him,

but his absence

touches my skin

into the blood

5.

Put your hand here —
on the morning of loss,
no chance to wave

goodbye in the air   Here
is the averted muscle
of the house disassembled

unstitched together,
the memory of his voice
a rip along the seam

6.

And then it's over.

No flowers.
No bears.
No candles.
No prayers.

Just a finger painting
soaking up a splash of water
on the bed tray.

And those brown hens standing in the rain
with no one left to care
about bringing them in.

Winter Light Slipping

There are perfumes fresh as infant's flesh
— Charles Baudelaire, *Correspondences*

The sleep-filled ones are still,
all lids and peace.
Competent conjurers they fill
their sweet-scented dreams
with fingers of light
quivering on the sill.

There is no history
weighing down the sun.
The language of the world
sings through as a swan —
lustrous as pearls.

On the other side of the glass
the blooms already pass.
One rose stands tough, its petals
pale and dewy.

In the midst of it we live without defense,
lean long into innocence.

Bird

This is for you, sweet mocking,
who have tasted how the wind sings,

who knows how slight a cloud weighs
on a sturdy post of light,

how, at night, the still lake of water
comes alive in our dreams, lapping.

In your song, love bird,
you have known primordial power

of forest creatures inside a flash of wings,
how mirror-bellies of leaping fish

can explode a world.
Read the tune placed in your beak

where the lust of one tear holds
every note of joy, of sorrow

trembling under the stars. Sing it back
with your opened plumes that sweep the moon,

fan every island of heaven.
You once said a desperate love

prone in the shadows equals everything.
If a lone feather touches it we feel

the ripple, the moan, the blood
beating forth a momentary forever.

So momentary. Here in the garden, bright
peering eyes move through a jungle of flowers.

Those flowers sense everything you sing.
They burst above the green, nourished

by longing until your song is done.
Waves of music echo through the heart's drumming rain.

Flight

The path to the west is smooth
We fly through slanted rays of light
into the arms of clouds that reach for us
like angels, though some are destined to fail

Our wings do not whip in the wind
but cut through air over cliffs and falls,
over azure peaks and flatlands. We ride
a stallion tripped by nothing, racing

to the finish line of swaying leaves,
dogs and deer. Headstrong horse of
horizons plowing through air of ice,
over the slow-moving patchwork planet,

faces sleep aisle to aisle, dream
release from your metallic throat.
Pegasus! Sea Biscuit! Savage-eyed
carrier of hope. Where do we begin,

where leave off?

Slow Shadow / White Delirium

From the sunlit meadow
flew the silver apparition
of the lost one found

free to wander at last
the cool blue mountains
above the greening trees

shed of crystals, sighing
in the wind. Wanderer
of the Eastern Sierras

maker of music of crimson
chimes and springs,
your gaze reaches us

from planted earth to
moons sailing in arches
as the backs of lovers do

in astonished youth —
brazen angels delicately
entwined, rocking, meditating

the deep red of lips,
the music of madness
before the aging flesh

Now you are dew dripping
from Columbine and Needlegrass
from Virgin's Bower and Locoweed

You are fire rising in sparks
to the breathless bowl of stars
as we, earthbound beneath this

slow shadow, white delirium,
sip upon the sour sweetness,
sing your words as tolling bells,

drunk with the clear nectar
of you, the angelic voice
carried in the bristlecone,

in the naked flight of birds —
red shouldered hawk
house finch,
thrasher

Burying the Dead

You are the slow shadow falling,
        white delirium spread above
darkened space,

a bird of many colors passing
        branch to branch
peering down

Your movement lifts in layers
from the nest,
        the braided grasses
brittle in the bough

in search of the upward force
        the new growth
off the ground
        into the unknown place

You said
        mountain
                mist
                        damselfly

speak tantalizing languages

And what is your language now
released from this world?

Perhaps the song is the sound
of deer nibbling across this field

or the condor dragging his shadow
over maidenhair
        That's more like it

We will know when we look at the moon
whether you left in ire
or peace

and we will wonder how we endured
your pres/absence
the entanglement of wax flowers and weeds
gasping in the heat

After a Short Summer

After a short summer
giving each other oceans, we part
with frost on our limbs.

III

Wolf Spider

1.

Our home is an intimate ocean. Translucent amber
            pours past the carpet roses, lavender,
finds us floating on the crests
of everyday routine

Together we adore the dogs, deal the cards,
            simmer in the chilled night air under planets
                        moving in harmony.
The surgeon will see you Thursday
and we joke   Nothing will happen because
            no one
wants to deal with me

Tonight a wolf spider camps in that crack
            between ceiling and wall, the kind of spider
that doesn't bother to build a web but   darts
            to its prey and pounces

I think of your fear.
Look for a shoe to smash it with.
You're lying on your back, one arm flung
over my pillow, mouth open, chest rising and falling
like a bay tide under moonlight
beaming through our hard work.

                        Forgive me, Love,
                        I just can't do it.

2.

The world smells of gold grass
baking under the sun. Above the house
turkey vultures swirl their invisible track,

wait for the merest stirring to end

The hour seems frozen, yet clothes continue
        thumping in the dryer. Dogs nap,
twitch on the bed.

It is all unknown

3.

The surgeon's eyes cast nets of dread. She pulls
the sonogram from its sheath. Her words
       leap on us
What bothers me most
we hang suspended
              is that the tumor
between life and death
         looks like a spider
Cells line up like hairy legs, reach
      in every direction
               no end in sight
We are paralyzed in airless air.
Our spirits stumble toward each other,
begin their navigation away
from the sickle of her tongue,
the quicklime of her sentence.

You sit on the edge of the table,
legs dangling over the disappearing floor.
We think *There has been a mistake.*

4.

Draped in moonlight
we lie on soft flannel
      Skin to skin
      Breast to breast

Some good signs over the weekend:
      Walking on the dock,
            a comet.
      In the morning, a snowy egret walked across our path,
      four flew overhead.
      Anything!

5.

This morning exhaustion remains smudged
under your eyes. Wondering
has become a stalker.

Yesterday I let sightings of comets and egrets
carrying me like a good dream. Today I lean
against the memory of your voice and,
yes, your golf shirts hanging in the closet.

I lean into the smell of you. Come home.
I thought I was stronger than this.

6.

Infiltrating lobular carcinoma
Twelve centimeters at least
Lymphatic involvement
No healthy tissue found
anywhere

And then cancer in all things.
The rising sun is a breast inflamed,
the moon a spot on the x-ray
of black sky

Every dream is pricked by long needles
And then New York, the world's nine-one-one.
You say it put things in perspective,
your own life   so small

The pain of the world allows you to weep
when you cannot cry for yourself.
This is the way of women.
There is no metaphor here,
only melting

7.

The honeybee in Spanish lavender
The green Adirondack chairs placed
                just so
The carnival-faced pansies turned
upwards, turned pockets of light.
The world is all buzz and sit and smile.

It could make one cry, all this progress
when the sun is high and the hedges leave
just a trace
of shadow.

And I think I may. Before you come home
and I'm snagged by that slightly tilted

gash in your smile, the wounds in our eyes
meeting like thieves in full daylight.

Perseid From a Park Bench

Moonless August night
laying head to head on our backs
Meteor   Meteor

Did you make a wish?

We humans do this,
place hope on a ball of dust
passing through a comet's tail
Dross

The same wish I always make

But I'm thinking of the silver maple that crowns our house
How, after a neighbor's dog slaughtered a doe
and left her to rot for weeks in her shade,
turkey vultures landed one by one
in her long leafy branches, lifted off,
circled our house for hours, their shadows
filling all the windows. I couldn't hide.
First to go were her eyes.

Good health for you

Silver maple launch pad   Squirrels
leapt from her arms onto our sun room,
showed their silver bellies through glass
At night stars posed on her slimmest shoots
before floating slowly to the horizon

Did the doctor say when we'd have the results?

Once, a family of wild turkeys hopped
from tree to glass to roof
and down again
except for one baby who called his fear of heights
alone on the edge

Was it before or after our initial conversations
of *tree goes tree stays*
that she began spearing our roof with heavy broken branches?
Wrong move, in either case

Meteor   Meteor

From June through October I've walked through our silent home
cool and laughing at the strained hum
of our neighbor's air conditioner
I've lain back at peace under the green

       Protected

So much for wishes   The tree is coming down
What to do with all that blue
With the fire burning through
No wishes left for the maple
but one, always the same one,
for you

Water Becomes Us

We wander the tangled meadow
of a newly birthed common,
spring in our blood, the taste of spring

on our skin, in our hair. Spring is in
the songs of the wending words
floating between us, words taken

from the latest film, the latest book, the news.
We give each other the music of our mouths,
hard land crunching beneath our heels,

note the young trees with their first blooms.
For decades I have watched you — young girl
in a frilly dress belted by guns and holsters —

leap from the blue bridge into the Niagara.
Your determination was a lovely dive,
a dare, your platinum hair an unwilling

accessory to grace. As you flew off
between paper mill and docks, I climbed hills
backwards to face the bay, my Golden Gate.

We hadn't met, of course, but I thought
I heard you say, *Lean into me like a wave.*
We rode the water as the water wanted —

smooth at times, then rough. Stars landed their light
on the slick deep blue of it
or turned to us their black backs.

We walk and I say *The apple blossoms of young trees
fade so soon,* but you are in the middle of a story
pulling a girl to shore, pulling me, those falls

roaring in the distance, and I know,
as that water always knew, something about
electricity, how we'd go over together.

Moonrise

The fog lying in over the mountains
is black. Is lined with ice. Is its own
mountain of snow.

Ten p.m. One planet to the southwest
shimmers copper and rose.
The mockingbird is silent as the night

lights up like day and the moon asks
who is braver.

We are small and so is every quandary.
By the time we walk indoors we are at peace
again. Not much else matters.

That and knowing the end will not be so bad,
that there is no difference, really, between
one shroud and the next,

be it mist, or veil or shadow. When we are tangled
in moon and meadow, a season of drowning
in light. Violet. Green. Silver

White Rose

—for D.B.

You open the door and re-enter the world.
The world knows not of your loss.
It just goes on. How can this be?
Morning mist has evaporated beneath the sun,

starlight has been covered with blue,
and you, suddenly motherless,
wander in air, reaching, reaching
and find she's not there. *Where?*

A Zen master wrote to me in a time of grief
a white rose worn in public reveals a mother has died,
know this when you see me.
Be gentle.

So many years ago and yesterday, too,
I wore one on my blouse. That master
gave me a secret name. Today I share it,
and a white rose with you:

Summer at the Winter Table

—for Gretchen

Just a trickle tickling through.
A fade of moss, but silent still

Black-and clear-winged damselfly,
butterfly, ferns longing for spring

Up the hill, over the path, a startled tree
lies collapsed, its mid-life caught in a crutch

of boughs. Windless,   breathless
afternoon. Birds small as thumbs

conference in the bays. Even in flight
each feathered body is an anchor to earth.

Do you hear those whistles of love from space?
They are calling you, if only we

can let go.

I want to become pure Love, you said.

Yes

Go

(Stay)

Go

Wrap us fleetingly, then

fly

There is so much freedom there from bones.

The Dawn is a Mirror of Myself

After the painting by Lawrence Ferlinghetti, 1994

Not just any dawn — a San Francisco dawn,
the sun blushing through the soft burn
of fog floating low over the water

between the Isle of Angels and North Beach bohemia.
It's time to tune in to a silver waltz
or something slower, to allow our bodies

what they wish most, to ease back with nowhere
but here, wings folded beneath the canvas,
sated from dreams of love and sublimity —

the whole scene a breathless hush of rose
and release — a tidal wave of it —
recorded for time. Dawn's skin,
made of earth and heaven, warms —
is perfectly moist
to the touch

Super Moon

Tonight's super moon will appear to be 14 percent bigger and 30 percent brighter than normal full moons as it takes its closest pass to earth all year.

— SF Chronicle, May 12, 2012

The glare of moon waxed golden-white
withering life of the sun
The sea turned silver beneath her rays
— Venetian glass slow-blown and spun

Flowers bloomed to bright mirrored eyes
focused on night's restless fingers
Not one shadow was left to mourn
where the snow-haired goddess lingered

Double mountain-glow aloft in midnight air,
blood's a-tremble beneath that burning face
where bodies braid in sweet baked grass — bare
in their perigee, their orbit through space

This night there is no sentence for lovers
No disgrace for quick hearts embraced
Intimate rooms and pathways hover
high over the sludge of fear's black waste

The moon is reached with keen cupped hands,
held there at it's brightest. *Morning will understand,*
you say. *If not, then morning be damned!*

Rock. Love. Stone. Loss.

One made from the other
One naturally formed,
the other designed

One started as magma
held beneath the surface,
heated in the dark

Out of view, it bubbles
into sensitive fingers, surges
to a cadenced pulse

Up, up. Pressure and heat
of intricacy brings a break
in the blazing skin

Just enough to burst through,
to cool and lose itself
particle by particle,

metamorphic hardness,
eons to smooth or bury
where it lays on the bottom

of the cold river bed
Enough sediment gathered
stacks for a wall.

Aloha Mele

Horizon to horizon
ocean winds howl,
dismantle petals faded

The throat of the pine's dress
shifts with light and life
Needles blister with music

Diaphanous wings fold
in the quenched hive of solitude
Only thoughts mill around

and incense driven air
— phantasmagoric balm —
sharing dreams inside

late kissed leaves
The bud, the bloom
advancing towards you

Under our feet
planet route and reel
We step forth o'er
the spin
say
Be still
impossibility

Return love directly
to the veins
Remember the beat of it
and beat again

Which is how?

Peer downward into the sky
float outside your dreams

You won't shatter

though a little red may burn
beneath the grass

Leilani
Kailani
   strong
love-limbed girl
accountable only to green, to blue
       fruitful boughs pitched in moonlight

once carried off
in umbra

Take note of your wings'
passion and farewell

The evening is laid out
corner to corner with greening light
The ocean passes over
the shores firm body

gentle-handed

Motion beneath us
        Motion above

Mea' aloha —
        mea' aloha
Afloat in naked beauty
        swirl'd mist
Kiss to a shell,
kiss to a kiss

Turned tenderly
        toward
together

Unchecked breath unbound
We are the pair
with silken nests on the flower
                       lokelani,
 ohia lehua

Children at play
busted out of the deep
dark
ravine
   of melancholy

Come   Your shining face
will not die in my arms

Aloha   mele —
flight of steam of exhalation
The bell rings this:
There is becoming
beyond the surround
becoming

Neither Selfness
nor monotone darkness
curled cowardice
or fantasies left

Some kernel of
Some scent of
joy

Orison, orison
Listen to the little breeze,
lei'd companion of sun,
sailing forth over hibiscus,
over slow lava flow

What we need for mele, aloha,
midnight rattle of coconut fronds   Warm wind-shaken
from roots to sky   Husk   Husk   The sun's
hot hands brushing the skin of hours —
salt, sand, sea   A ceiling of stars posed
in the door of lava caves, or fallen
to the balcony of light   dark   light

Torch-flickered paths revealing
birds of paradise, pulsating drums —
hula hips swaying touch taste love
here on heaven's shore — the space for living
wide open under the sky

Aloha   aloha
     mea' aloha

to your hands
to your breath
to your flight
to our momentary moon
                    mahina
Baby birds unafraid to open

to swoop and hoard
  even the smoke
    as it rises
      gently
        from the bed of your black stream hair
                moku, ipo
                moku, ipo

your lips
  your lips
    your breast
      your belly
        your blood

Aloha, hour of sighs
                aloha
We are still being born
at last
                into scattered light
receding
        like the sea
        into the sea

Honu,
            Honu,
                    Humuhumunukunukuapuaʻa

Aloha, mea'
Aloha

IV

Topaz Lake

By the time we reached Marblemount
We considered them well broken
 — Kenneth Rexroth, "A Real Pearl"

At sixteen I rode south on the Van Ness bus,
got a job as a typist for a modeling agency boss,
typed contracts in the reception room
while she, with her bleached flip and heels
named after a certain knife, chewed tobacco,
spit into the urn next to my chair.
She never missed. She picked her girls carefully
from the long line of jaded mothers' dreams.
Some she taught how to walk, how to enter a car
knees pressed together, how to position their arms
when a gentleman puts on, takes off their coats.
Others she sat in front of magnified mirrors
with a dime store counter of Cody and Revlon,
commanded them to pick up the tweezers,
pull out their brows, pencil on replacements
to perfection. After a year of typing name, address,
age, height, weight, bust, hips, hair color,
cost, cost, cost, she called me to that table,
said my lessons would be free. Now pluck.
One, two, maybe three hairs and I was done
with the pain. That night, waiting for the forty-two
Van Ness, one of her models smiled her perfect
face smile — her name was Judy and she was the most
beautiful woman I'd ever seen, except for Sister Roseanna —
and told me Don't ever model for Miss V, she takes us
to big lawyers parties, others, do you understand?
At sixteen I rode the bus south down Van Ness.
I got a job as a typist for the biggest madam in San Francisco.
And then I quit. Today I sit by a lake in Antelope Valley
and think of all the edges approached, crossed, not crossed.
The day is a large bowl of silence scented with virgin grass.
The emerald bed of April holds me in peace.
I hope Judy got away.

The Day in Silence Under One Burning Star
Guerneville, California

Came the day when we watched the river,
when we walked the woods
breathing, observing, sauntering
west county world thus

Old men in hip waders, licenses
clipped to their hats, mourn the absence
of fish. Not a hat, but a basket for flowers
on his head. "The green on the ducks
is so much brighter here than the birds in Golden Gate Park."

Mallards dive and dive, raise to the surface,
shake like labradors. They swim the clear current,
break through light dancing in place. There is nothing
amiss. Not the gold leaves dropped or the
mistletoe bunched in nude branches. Behold
the emerald crimson clear flowing world.
Even the small dog crosses his paws, gazes
in silence. An animal knows paradise,
fish or no.

But for one golden drop on the redwood tree
where would nature be. Redwoods shine with
yesterday's rain. Moist, cool moss,
mushrooms, the warm orb shining softly
through the trees. Ravens speak across the canopy
from deep in their throats. Once a woman
felt the sun blissfully, laid across its voluptuous,
pulsing print and napped. Like old times, faerie times,
every tree an altar to vertigo, lawlessness and flight
(knock on wood!). Tender world of little streams,
of little tongues speaking ancient identities,
we sing as mockingbirds sing, always bursting forth.

Ode to the Moo Cow
— North of the Gate

O Moo Cow
ankles stuck in the muck
of winter, your pink milkies

the opposite of tufa —
over the green sea of grass,
over the clover depths

and expectant naked trees,
a two-wheeler trips in the sky
puffs a vapor trail over

the mating tail of a great white crane
To be born a bird
or a small plane in flight

or you, dear Moo,
is to know there is no labor
in being beautiful

Beneath the whistling sun
you travel through full peace,
over the land all our sight can reach,

those unending images of bog-meadow,
buttercup-gilded hills, green elegance
of earth's wide heart and release
and you eating it up

Café Paradelle

In the Flying Goat everyone is a vagrant.
In the Flying Goat everyone is a vagrant.
Newspapers read as if the world gives a damn.
Newspapers read as if the world gives a damn.
Everyone is flying in the goat world. As if read,
the damn newspaper gives a vagrant a

Conversation overheard: Let me finish where I was going.
Conversation overheard: Let me finish where I was going.
Love, I believe you most when your mouth is closed.
Love, I believe you most when your mouth is closed.
Let me mouth *you* when most believe conversation is *I*.
I overheard love going, where I was your finish.

Outside, red leaves rattle lost love through the trees.
Outside, red leaves rattle lost love through the trees.
The first blue day without clouds brings a sudden chill.
The first blue day without clouds brings a sudden chill.
Lost blue clouds rattle red without the trees. Outside
Brings the first sudden day through a chill love leaves.

The blue vagrant mouth brings a love conversation.
Clouds believe you, the first red lost day gives in, is a rattle
Without world. Outside your sudden flying leaves everyone
I. Let me read love trees, finish through the overheard.
Goat closed, newspaper, where most is a damn chill
When the I was going, *as if*.

Ingenium

New East Span, San Francisco-Oakland Bay Bridge

Over the bay's wind-blossomed body,
a soaring of light and motion. Newborn
might made of dreams and well-worn knees.

The sky casts off her old gray dress for a plume,
blithe and mad with beauty —a cool white life
wrapped in silver air. Behold the sleek rachis

rising on the backbone, its white vanes a gleam
in Oakland's lovely eye. Breath of Yemanja
brushes through, brushes through. How quickly

this bridge becomes a part of it all, mingles
with the flow — the sails below, the breeze
wandering along its piers — pursues its flight

into clear, Elysian atmosphere. Muse, lyre,
feather and wing, raised to our eyes you bring
radiance. Hold us in your elegant arms,

carry us over the world solidly, no sudden
gaps to mind, no trapdoors. No trolls. Just
angels thick as under-sky, here on the inland sea.

Note: The word *engineer* is from the Latin root *ingenium*,
meaning "cleverness." "Yemanja," in the Yoruba religion, is the
ocean, the essence of motherhood, and a protector of children.

Haiku Clouds

Inside the blue eye
clouds like the ocean, the wind
Lone, pale survivors

Soft tremulous light
A wingéd shape's rapid keel —
White, star-bright gesture

Lawny spring mountain
Moonlike blooms breathe high above
ever-changing notes

See the shattered mast
crouched in the sky's agony?
Flap of ribboned sails?

Sometimes a shroud draped
over the rocks of despair
mirrors the dark night

The white plumed womb
births soft showers into air
One swan's liquid wing

All day the clouds sing
under a sun like summer
a song high and vast

Sky's purest children
form moonlike blooms overhead,
fetch myriad dreams

Orion by the agate sea,

by the drive where the old dogwood tree
stands with raucous birds in her hair
and spider fairies sail into the wind

Orion in your backdrop of solid crows
where the moon climbs through plums
and shimmering scales of robins sleep
waiting for the sun's slick tongue —

the rip of darkness, the opening of its veins,
the pulse of dreams rustling like straw —
you witness everything — a woman's body
delineated by wind and silk moving smoke,

a lone man in a yellow window
counting dreams,
the ways that sunlight falls.

Everything We Read

Darkness at the door. Someone down.
A lament of casings rustle along the curb.

Break the bread, pass the policemen.
The moon stares with empty eyes.

The end is less than a hair.
Less than a feather floating up.

Just a sentence beneath an ad.
The bottom corner of the seventh page.

In blue waters, young men mirrored.
They have traveled the underground rivers

of blood blooms everlasting, media sniff-
sniffing at the color line. Good short story,

the count. Enough to strike the fear in, enough to
nail the lie in.   Just.

Genius does not grow in newspapers.
Little as we know, we know you

not at all, have forgotten conveniently the
connection of sacred roots entwined,

all of us in our cells composed
of universe, our atoms used, re-used

millions of times. In baffled oneness
ghosts drift quietly, gaze down through

the rattling of wind through bones,
the tender knitting of earth.

In Memory of Oscar Grant

New Years Day, 2009

As the young supermarket worker lay facedown
amid the darkness
as he lay there in Oakland's underground,
where moon and stars are barred
unarmed, black, pinned down,
inside the darkness
begging not to be shot,
as he lay there covered with cops
dark forms with dark wings
hiding him from view as best they could,
through fear's thick veil
cell phones up and down the tracks
shape-shifting transit crowd
recorded the cop pulling his gun,
pressing it to the back of the unarmed black man
strength in meekness
who was a young friend, who was a lover,
as a drop of dew
who was a father laying facedown
as a small drop of dew

As the young black man lay there,
encircled
pinned down, facedown, begging,
a lone drop of dew
a cop shot him in the back, BAM!
dying
shot him in the back!

As the young unarmed man laid dying,
birds within the wind
cops hiding him the best they could,
fish within the wave
cell phones recorded the shooting of Oscar Grant,
thoughts of man's own mind
unarmed,
float through
pinned down,
all above
face down,
begging.
the grave

Everyone saw it and saw it and saw it
those eyes burn through
and no one can say

Death!
it wasn't so.
The last embrace

The Fox

"It's typical for only one of three fox pups to make it."
Volunteer, Wildlife Rescue

What if, instead of seeing the kit in the yard
rummaging for food, nuzzling his mother,
you found him lifeless, being ripped
by vultures? What if you had to go to a neighbor
asking for help to remove the carcass

and when you walked back to the yard
there was nothing there — not a bone or even
a bit of blood — as if it was all in your mind.
What if the kit's only living sibling — the runt —
came out from under the shed, seemingly

motherless and hungry. What if you were told
it's too dark for anyone to rescue him so you
feed him berries intending to bring out water,
kibble, but the mother is back roaring
from the fence-top so you drop the berries,

retreat. What if you try to sleep but can't
because the berries may not be enough to sustain
the kit overnight, mother or no mother,
so you get up at two and bring kibble and water.
Finally you sleep. And what if in the morning,

after watching them through the window
drink and eat and eat and drink until the mother
leaves for the day and the baby goes back under
the shed, you walk outside and the carcass is back,
picked clean, one pile of leg bones, the curved

spine and ribs nearby. This time you don't go for help
but get your gloves and a plastic bag and, between
the flies and the wasps, pick up each bone
carefully, remembering what they looked like when
they were connected and covered with fur, gallivanting

on the deck, not a worry in the world. What if?
No matter. There's a runt under the shed, three bowls
on the deck: Water. Kibble. Berries.

Stroke

This is the mother's ruined body. Her body
paralyzed into a five-year slumber. Her body
not buried but dead, still. Even her toes
dead for the voyage of one red orb
drunken-winged in her brain.

These were her deep red roses she bent
her knees to, cared for with sharp steel weapons,
smoke streaming from her mouth. Her words
fell on the doctor's ears like insects. He swatted
her home where she waited for the storm
to come or to pass. It left her with half a body.
Her body paralyzed in a five-year death.

These are the mother's strange brown eyes
telepathing her SOS, her silent shriek, her terror.
She cleaves to the daughter for salvation
from this diving bell sinking.

This is the daughter's own voice that can save
nothing, change nothing, but wrap the mother
up, fly her to a nest of keepers, her body body-cuffed
between rails, her body waiting for death to take
its god damned time. A woman, yet
from these tears, a girl again, in this university
of gated roads leading to …

Mirror Image

for T.W

.

We have been friends in the glass
for almost thirty years. A type of
two-way class in love and Zen
with an aside of hair. *It's time* you said,
when it became too long for care.
We reminisced as the scissors snipped us
back to our 1980s brush-cut beginnings.
Between then and now how many confidences,
questions asked and answered?
In my mother's day, women went weekly.
For her, it was Herbert every Thursday.

It had little to do with beauty.

You revealed your loves, I revealed mine.
You married, had children, dogs, sheep, music,
and a long list of *do you know so and so*.
(I never did.) Mostly, you had a free and
open heart. A few days ago, at just fifty,
it stopped. While you lie in a coma,
we pace, unable to find sleep or a comb.
When we look in the mirror no one is there
but hundreds of weeping women —men, too —
the feeling of hands resting on their shoulders.
Six weeks you said, as we hugged goodbye.

Sélectif

When you come past my window
Bless me
For my light still burns
                — Shu Ting

It had everything and nothing
to do with aging the day I came to

the poet's house recorder in hand.
She sat up in bed, the whole room soft

with fabric draped over every surface;
a muffled world mostly blue.

Question after question was asked
and as the answers were trapped in her

throat, if they made it that far,
silence was recorded, larger and louder

each time. Her eyes, too, seemed to grow
with each unknowing of a life lived

thunderously between here and Paris.
Perhaps she could read her poems instead?

"Silly girl," she said. The *Collected* spread
across her lap, she glanced at the page,

raised her radiant face to the ceiling,
an innocent waking to naked light, and recited

from memory poem after poem after poem.
A light somewhere between white and yellow

emanated from the top of her head, became a flower
singing. She was a real American beauty.

Doppelganger, Bryce Canyon

In memory of G. L.

Today I saw you walk toward the rim.
You wore a lavender jacket, earth-trimmed.
In your right hand you carried a notebook,
your left tucked warmly away. As you took

each step closer to the edge of the world
you seemed to think how long the days grow,
how useless to worry. In mountain cold
you examined bird nests, stubborn patches of snow,

black fingers of far-off rain suspended
in the sky. You wrote in your notes *blue grouse,
hermit thrush, ponderosa pine.* And then
you stood on the ledge, arms open loud,

unwilling to let this or any canyon
close you in. Instead, you looked down at those
fantastic shapes, matched the pull of them,
waited for the moon to re-light the rust, rose

of the mute city's ancient paralysis,
the raven's soaring rock to tree. Then this:
When I turned back, you were gone,
those hoodoos flaming darkly toward dawn.

I Wish You Hens and Chickens

Beauty for ashes may I give alway:
I'm sure I shall not pass again this way
(Anonymous)

A cure for what ails you
lies in the hand of a corpse
Lay it on

Hot and cold flashes disappear
if you drape a bag of spiders
'round your neck

To cure a headache, wrap your head
with the corner of a sheet that was once
wrapped around a corpse

Or, if you're luckier,
a sack of warm potatoes
for tonsillitis

To rid yourself of fever
lie on a beach near high tide
Receding waves will carry it away

Always beware of redheads
and whistling girls of any hair color

May a white lamb with the sun on its face
greet you in early morning

I Confess

It is lovely to live where one
Doesn't need to write of snow in spring,
Where so many days are a perfection of blue.
Oh don't sniff like that —
You'd love it too.
But this isn't about the weather,
Per se, but about the one cloud
Making its lonely excursion, too small
To cast a shadow on a single poppy.
It's illegal to pick that wild flower,
The State flower the quail peck through,
Their funny hats and popping talk
Laughable and lovely, too.
I wouldn't say no to a crepe right now.
Something sweet and slightly nutty.
I used to sit in my old wooden rocker
On the second floor of my Mission studio
Drinking brandy and smoking cigars —
Uptons, I think they were called
Then I graduated to pipes with cherry tobacco
From Seaport Village in San Diego.
The room had windows on three walls
For watching the moon float over
22nd street to the corner bodega.
Sometimes my downstairs neighbor would climb the fire escape
To rap on my window with a Corona. She was just out
of some asylum for murdering her mother. She could
Fill that crepe and more. Today isn't yesterday,
Except for a little. Truth be told I miss the fog
living here in the warm mornings, noons and nights
sweeping around the winery roads on my Vespa
called Ciao Bella, feeling years younger
Than I am or will ever be again. Last weekend
We found a squirrel's tail lying on our deck.
Talk about alone.

NOTES:

"Aloha Mele:
"Aloha" has several meanings: "hello," "goodbye" and "love" are three.
"Honu" is the green sea turtle
"Humuhumunukunukuapua'a" is the Hawaiian state fish
"Kailani" is a girl's name meaning "Sea and Sky"
"Leilani" is a girl's name meaning "Heavenly Flowers"
"Lokelani" and "ohia lehua" are two official flowers of Hawaii, one from the Big Island of Hawaii, one from Maui
"mahina" means "moon" and "moonlight"
"mea' aloha" means "beloved"
"Mele" means "song"

"Café Paradelle":
The paradelle is a form invented by Billy Collins to *parody* strict forms, especially the villanelle. He claimed that it is a rigorous French fixed form first appearing in eleventh century love poetry with four six-line stanzas in which the first and second lines, and the third and fourth lines of the first three stanzas, are identical; the fifth and sixth lines, which traditionally resolve these stanzas, use *all* of the words from the preceding lines and *only* those words; and the final stanza uses *every* word from *all* the preceding stanzas and *only* those words.

"Fallen Leaves" and "Small Angels in the Mirror":
On December 14, 2012, 20 children and 6 adults were fatally shot at Sandy Hook Elementary School in Newtown, Connecticut.

"I Wish You Hens and Chickens":
Italicized lines from "I shall not Pass Again This Way," Anonymous; and anonymous Irish blessings

"Stroke":
"A (wo)man, yet by these tears…" from "Sea Drift,", Walt Whitman

KATHERINE HASTINGS is the author of *Cloud Fire* (Spuyten Duyvil 2012) and several chapbooks. She is the editor of *What Redwoods Know — Poems from California State Parks,* which was sold as a benefit for the California State Parks Foundation. She is the executive director of the non-profit *WordTemple*; host of WordTemple on NPR affiliate KRCB FM, and curator of the WordTemple Poetry Series and WordTemple Arts & Lectures in Sonoma County, CA. Hastings grew up in the Cow Hollow neighborhood of San Francisco and received her MFA in Writing from Vermont College. She lives in Sonoma County, CA. For more information go to www.wordtemple.com and www.krcb.org/wordtemple.

SPUYTEN DUYVIL
Meeting Eyes Bindery
Triton
Lithic Scatter

Made in the USA
Charleston, SC
13 June 2014